Praise for other books by Peter Burwash:

Praise for *Improving the Landscape of Your Life:*

"Every once in a while, a really interesting read comes my way and strikes a chord. Peter Burwash has done just that. This is a man who really cares and who really wants to make a difference. And he does. His book is a blend of practical wisdom and depth of experience to teach us how to take charge in every aspect of our lives."

-Lee Iacocca

Praise for *The Key to Great Leadership:*

"Inspirational and compelling bite-size quotes illustrated by motivational stories on two key competitive advantages of the future—service and leadership."

-Dr. Steven Covey,
Chairman of Covey Leadership Center and
Author of *The Seven Habits of Highly Effective People*

"If something's not going right, *The Key* will impact your thinking on all elements of leadership. Its reminders are the ingredients of leading."

-Peter V. Ueberroth,
Time Magazine's Man of the Year

Praise for *Total Health*:

"It's to your own good that you have picked up *Total Health*. Read it, and heed its wise and compassionate counsel, and you will be well on the way to a new level of aliveness, healing, and joy."

-from the foreword by John Robbins,
Author of *Diet for a New America*,
Founder of EarthSave International

"Peter again serves an ace with *Total Health*. He has been a role model for me for years and this book exceeds even my lofty expectations. No one can fail to benefit from time spent with Peter Burwash's approach to life, and *Total Health* is Peter."

-Howard F. Lyman, J.D.
President, International Vegetarian Union

"Mr. Burwash presents a collection of 'life lessons' . . .with the wisdom and compassion of a teacher who's 'been there.' This sage guidance on achieving *Total Health* is a gift—for your body, for your spirit, and for the health of the entire planet."

-Michael A. Klaper, M.D. Director, Institute of
Nutrition, Education, and Research
Author, *Vegan Nutrition, Pure & Simple*

Dear Teenager,

IF YOU ONLY KNEW...

Dear Teenager,

IF YOU ONLY ONLY KNEW...

PETER BURWASH

TORCHLIGHT
PUBLISHING

First Printing 2000

Cover design by Yamaraja Dasa
Interior design by Christopher Glenn / Glenn Graphics
Printed in India at Indira Printers, New Delhi-110 020

Published simultaneously in the United States of America and Canada by Torchlight Publishing, Inc.

Library of Congress Cataloging-in-Publication Data

>   Burwash, Peter.
>   Dear teenager : if you only knew— / by Peter Burwash
>   p.   cm.
>   ISBN 1-887089-20-9 (cloth)
>   I. Teenagers. 2.Parent and teenager. I. Title.
>
>   HQ796.B838 2000
>   305.235—dc21   99-054679

Attention Colleges, Universities, Corporations, Associations and Professional Organizations: *Dear Teenager: If You Only Knew* is available at special discounts for bulk purchases for fund-raising or educational use. Special books, booklets, or excerpts can be created to suit your specific needs.

Torchlight Publishing, Inc.

For more information, contact the Publisher.
PO Box 52
Badger CA 93603
Email: torchlight @spiralcomm.net
www.torchlight.com

Dedication

*This book is dedicated to all my
teachers during my teenage years.
Thank you for persevering with a
student who struggled.
And to my Dad, who passed away
while I was writing this book.
He personified honesty, integrity
and humility.
He was my hero.*

Acknowledgments

I would like to thank my wife, Lynn, and my two daughters, Kimberly and Skyler, who afforded me the quiet time to write this book on a secluded island in the South Pacific. My sincere thanks also to Alister Taylor, the best publisher an author could have, and to Susanne Bolte, whose superb attention to detail as an editor was so helpful.

Contents

Contents

Foreword

As a parent, teacher, counselor, and social worker, I have seen families at their heroic best and most painful worst. Over the last thirty years I have had the privilege of working with hundreds of teens and their parents to heal broken bonds, establish communications, and generally help create a healthy environment from which kids could be launched into productive and fulfilling adulthood.

Needless to say, as a professional I have read countless books and referred parents and educators to study a myriad of "How To. . ." and inspirational literature in an attempt to instruct and thereby change the often difficult dynamics between adults and teens.

This wonderful offering by Peter Burwash uniquely addresses the teenager directly. Peter comes alongside the reader with frankness, keen insight, and a place of genuine respect. *Dear Teenager* speaks to the intelligence, emotions, and soul of the teenage reader and promises to be an invaluable companion to any young person who is fortunate enough to receive it at one of the most exciting and important milestones on the journey of life.

Enjoy the read!

Ilene Tibbitts, M.A.
Marriage and Family Counseling

Chapter One

Being a Teenager:
A Major Turning Point

For many of you, your teenage years will define what the rest of your lives will look like. These years are definitely a major turning point in your lives. And it can be a very difficult, painful, and tumultuous transitional time. You are desperately struggling to find out who you are and where you are going. Some of you are wondering why you are even on this earth. Being a teenager has always been a challenge, but since the late 1960s, the hurdles, temptations, and confusing signals have made it extremely difficult to navigate the turbulent waters of the teenage years.

To understand why things magnified in their complexity, it is probably helpful to look at two factors that affected the 40-year period from around 1929 to 1969. In 1929, there was a major depression that occurred in the U.S. Within a month, powerful businessmen were bankrupt and were selling apples and newspapers on the streets. There were major shortages of necessary goods and money. Banks closed and millions lost their life savings. That experience taught the people of that era to avoid being caught off guard again. They saved and saved, both money and goods, just in case.

The second experience that affected the population was World War II from 1939-1945. Almost everything was rationed. Once again, there was a shortage of material goods. This, coupled with the sobering effect of loved ones being killed in the war, caused people to take care of and protect whatever they had. However, post-World War II brought an era of huge prosperity. Parents felt relatively safe and secure once again, and millions of children were born from 1945-1950. These are referred to as the "baby-boomers." These children saw their parents acquire a multitude of material goods—cars, televisions, electrical appliances. In addition, they expanded their bank accounts. Yet when these "baby-boomers" became teenagers, they were very perceptive. They saw that the acquisition of material assets was not making their parents any happier. And so began a major movement towards spirituality, or anti-materialism. Love and peace became the operative words of the late 60s. It was a period of re-awakening, a search for what would really make one happier. The downside of this era was the mass introduction of drugs, and with drugs came a whole new set of challenges for society, particularly for teenagers. Not only were teenagers faced with the peer pressures of alcohol, cigarettes, and sex, but along came another temptation or pseudo-escape in the form of drugs.

Couple these temptations with the explosion of violence on TV, in movies, and in everyday life, and the element of fear was multiplied, either through real or surreal experiences. As I began to write this book in 1998, there had just been a series of fatal shootings in schools across America. A few years earlier, metal detectors were introduced into many schools, as it was estimated that one million school children were taking guns to school each year.

On top of all this, there developed an unparalleled awareness among teenagers about the mass destruction and abuse of your home, the planet Earth. At no time has there been such disregard for Mother Earth as in the last century. When I was a teenager, I never knew what a rainforest was. Today almost every one of you not only knows about a rainforest, but understands its importance to all of us. How do we measure the impact of a society that is now so out of balance?

Amidst all of this, you hear many adults saying that teenagers of today are the worst ever. One headline that was splashed across the newspapers of the world recently came from a survey by Public Agenda (a company out of New York City). It said that 50% of the people polled felt that American kids are rude, lazy, and spoiled. And 71% felt that American teenagers are irresponsible. Yet you hardly ever hear adults lamenting to teenagers, "We are sorry that we have destroyed so much of your planet, polluted your air, poisoned your waterways, and wiped out most of your topsoil, making it difficult to find quality, tasty food to feed you." Nor do many adults apologize for producing such violent images on TV and in movies that you are afraid to walk the streets at night. Nor do they apologize for flashing vast numbers of advertisements in front of you that say, "Buy this, it will make you happier," thereby creating an illusory sense of happiness for you. The generation before you creates this environment and then wonders why you are not having such a great time here.

Now that you have been handed this platter of pollution, violence, and disillusionment, what can you do? Actually your choice is a simple one. You can continue to be part of the problem or part of the solution. You can either be angry and rebel, or you can work to change things. Mahatma Gandhi, who helped lead the country of India to independence in the 1940s, said something we can all learn from: "An eye for an eye makes the whole world blind." Far too many people have followed the philosophy of "an eye for an eye, tooth for a tooth." Nobody wins when you have a revengeful thought process.

Most adults look back on their teenage years and say, "I wish I had known then what I know now." Why? Because knowledge eliminates fear. And during your years as a teenager, there's so much anxiety and fear that some extra knowledge could go a long way to help you paddle through the waves of insecurity. Before writing this book, I spent thousands of hours listening to teenagers. In a way, it was quite painful; however, the pain came in a way that might surprise you. I am a very positive person, and even as a young kid I looked at the bright side of life. Yet I must admit that the years of 13-19 were ones that I had buried well back in my mind. Talking to your peers re-opened the painful times I had as a teenager. The more teenagers I talk to, the more I realize that there is not really a generation gap, just the packaging and storing of different perceptions of life. Your basic trials and tribulations are no different from mine or those of any other teenager before you. You feel the same awkwardness, confusion, sadness, and concern that most teenagers felt. However, if you live in the U.S. today, you must worry about whether the kid in the next locker has a gun, or if your best friend will commit suicide or get pregnant. Another important difference today, however, is that you live in a world of mass media that brings the latest global tragedy to you within minutes. Whereas teenagers of previous eras might have been shocked periodically with horrifying news, you get it almost daily. Then along comes the biggest pitfall of them all—hopelessness or despair. In the late 60s, there was a song that had the words, "What's it all about, Alfie?" I'm sure many of you are saying to yourselves, "What's it all about?" "Why am I here?" "What is my purpose?"

The fact that teenage suicides are rising rapidly is an indication that many of you are really struggling. As I write this book, I am hopeful that you will not perceive it as another adult trying to tell a teenager what to do. Ultimately, you will accept or reject what is written here on your own terms. Please understand that my only wish is that, as you read this book, you will do so with an open heart and open mind.

It is written so you won't have to bury your teenage memories like I did. Most of the valuable lessons I learned in life came after I was a teenager, but I sure could have used these lessons then.

How do we know some snakes are poisonous? Because some individual has died on our behalf. We do not have to pick up that snake, let it bite us, then see what happens. A fool learns from his own mistakes, but a wise person learns from the mistakes of others. So often you will find yourself saying to your parents, "But Mom, but Dad, I have to see for myself." That's not necessary. Save yourself the pain and suffering. Remember, knowledge eliminates fear.

In the ensuing chapters, we will focus on the understanding of many of the issues and challenges that your peers discussed with me over the last couple of years. Although there are a great many issues that concern you, the one that was most often discussed by you concerned your parents and your relationships with them. They had the greatest influence in your lives (whether it was negative or positive). Some of you loved the relationship, and others hated it.

You may have gotten the sense that this is a book that will be sympathetic to your challenges. You may want your parents to read it. In any effort to increase understanding, there has to be good communication. Hopefully, by you and your family and friends reading this book, you will be able to exit the teenage years with a whole new perspective on yourself as well as the world and people around you.

Major Issues for Teachers in the 1940s
Source: California Department of Education

1. Talking
2. Chewing gum
3. Making noise
4. Running in the halls

5. Getting out of line
6. Wearing improper clothing
7. Not putting paper in the waste basket

Major Issues for Teachers in the 1990s
My survey of teachers

1. Drugs
2. Weapons (guns, knives, explosives)
3. Anger of students
4. Apathy of students
5. Retaliation of students
6. Lack of parents' support in disciplining the students

Chapter Two

Understanding Your Parents

B eing a parent is the single most difficult job in the world, and for many moms and dads, this is just one of the many things they do. There are thousands of books written on the subject, and almost every week there is a newspaper column on how to deal with children.

Without question, the most challenging time for the majority of parents is the teenage years. It is the time when so many of you start rebelling against and challenging authority. Some of you exist in a state of constant mortification at the prospect of supervision by your parents.

Perhaps the best way to understand any situation is to put yourself in the other person's role. Can you imagine what it would be like to raise YOU? When I asked teenagers that question, most either laughed, giggled, or rolled their eyes, and a light bulb went on.

Almost unanimously, you agreed that it would be very difficult to raise you.

Writing this chapter would be easy if all parents were perfect. But they aren't perfect, and they never will be. When you were younger, you may have thought that your parents could do no wrong. But as you became more aware, you realized their faults. Now, a few of you may be reading this and saying, "But I really do have perfect parents." However, if you asked them if they were perfect, they would say no. They would have hundreds of mistakes to share with you.

The ideal parent/teenager relationship is one where there is very strong mutual respect, particularly when it comes to communication. Almost all problems between two people boil down to poor communication. You don't have to agree with someone's ideas or thoughts, but you must respect their right to communicate. The major challenge for some of you, however, is having to live and try to communicate with a parent who is permanently or temporarily unfit to be a parent. Ask any kid what it is like to grow up with a parent who is unhappy or unstable.

For example, if your parent is an alcoholic and goes into a rage (physically, mentally, or both) while drinking, there is virtually no opportunity (nor is it smart) to have any communication at all. It is tough to respect that kind of behavior.

When confronted with this situation, what are your options? None are what you may want. But for those of you who have parents who are physically violent, you may have to take drastic action. For years, spousal abuse was kept behind closed doors. Most women were afraid to bring this out into the open. Now, thousands of women are coming forth, and the same is true with children. More children, particularly teenagers, are exposing their parents for physical abuse. I know it's a tough decision, but your right as a human being is to not be physically abused.

Before going this route, however, I recommend that you make every attempt possible to understand the reasons for your parents' behavior. They may have been abused as children and know no other lifestyle. Or if they drink a lot of alcohol, understand why. Most people drink for taste or to become someone else. If it's for the latter reason, they most likely have some deep-rooted insecurities about themselves. And this is where you can potentially help. Many, many parents have quit drinking because of guidance from, support of, or insistence by their children. You often have more power or influence than you think. By showing your parents that you love them and that you care for their health, you can begin a much-needed dialogue. There is a popular phrase that says, "Kids don't care how much parents know until they know how much they care." Now you can reverse the role. Parents and children are here to teach one another in this lifetime.

Remember that a large number of parents are not confident in being a parent. Some of them have never really grown up themselves and remain "children" most of their lives. Some of them are overwhelmed by the responsibility of trying to raise you.

It also helps to understand that when you don't follow the rules and guidelines set down by them, they still have to co-exist with you. In a regular job, if you don't follow your leader, you're shown the exit door rather quickly. But in a family, this is not the appropriate action. Sure, your parents can throw you out of the house. But do you really think this is what they want in their hearts? They have nurtured you through your infancy and pre-teen years. Once you were this cuddly little baby and adorable kid who thought your parents could do no wrong. You idolized them, and they fell more in love with you. They have years of memories stored in their hearts. Do you really think they want to throw you out on the street?

Yet some of you have driven your parents to this depth of despair. To your parents, you may always be their "baby." Let them enjoy that thought.

A number of years ago, I took tennis instruction into prisons in America. Our company wanted to inject the positive activity into an otherwise tough situation. It became my favorite program, and I got to know many of the prisoners, some of whom were rehabilitated through our program and with whom I am very good friends today. What I learned from them was that 100 percent—not 99 percent—but 100 percent said they wished they had listened to their parents when they were younger. They also were unanimous in mentioning that they wished that their parents had instilled more discipline into their households.

In my communications with teenagers over the last couple of years, I found that those of you who were happiest and most successful in every respect were those who had been required to perform chores regularly while growing up. Success with smaller chores had inspired you to gradually try more challenging tasks. But sometimes in life, the timing is off. When you are quite young, you are often eager to help clean the dishes, yet you aren't strong enough or sometimes tall enough to perform the task, and your parents say, "When you get older you can help out with the dishes." But when you are older, doing dishes isn't something you really want to do. And here is where a change in your perspective can help.

Your parent spends one hour preparing a meal—the least you can do is be part of the team that spends ten minutes cleaning up the dishes. This is called APPRECIATION.

Let's talk about appreciation—it's the number one engine for human development. People thrive on it. Think about your relationship with your mom and/or dad. What have you done or do you do to show your appreciation for them? Think of the enormous sacrifices they have made and continue to make on your behalf. When was the last time you sent them a heartfelt card or letter? When did you make something truly special for them? Something that you were so excited to give them, which you could hardly wait for them to open? Ask not what your parents can do for you, but instead ask what you can do for your parents. You will notice an incredible difference in your relationship with them.

The more you show your appreciation for someone, the more you invite that person into your heart. And the more that happens, the more they will understand you. Understanding leads to respect, and respect leads to their listening to you.

I often joke that parents don't listen to their kids, yet part of this quip is very serious. Some parents, just like political or business leaders, abuse the privilege of their leadership role. They talk but don't listen to those whom they are leading.

Being a good leader means being a good listener, and being a good parent means being a good listener. Learning also necessitates listening or seeing. This listening is critical to your development in life. This means learning to listen to what people are saying without mentally composing your response while they are still speaking.

Watch your parents next time they are having an argument. While one is speaking, the other's lips are already wound up. I'm sure many of you do the same thing. Communication between parents and teenagers is often a power struggle of words.

When communicating with parents, show them the courtesy of listening. They may sometimes be irrational in their communication, but in most cases they are sincerely trying to help you. A famous quote from a father to a son goes as follows: "My son, treat everybody with politeness, even though there may be those who are rude to you—and remember, you show courtesy to others not because they are gentlemen, but because YOU are a gentleman."

One of the biggest frustrations teenagers have with their parents is the inconsistency of their actions and their directions to you. They tell you, "Do your homework," then they go turn on the TV, or "Don't smoke," as they light up another cigarette, or "Don't drink," as they sit there with a can of beer in hand. There is a quote that is very relevant here: "Children close their ears to advice and open their eyes to what parents do."

And then there is the most dreaded response from your parents: You are asked to do or not to do something because "I say so." If parents only realized that this drives you crazy! It isn't fair. This is where you have to make the effort to develop a rational level of communication with your parents. And here is where I offer you a suggestion—only a suggestion. (I promised myself in writing this book that I wasn't going to write with the goal of advising or directing you as a teenager. Instead, I hope this book will assist you in deciding how you can improve the quality of your own life.) Now the suggestion: Since our oldest daughter was around four years of age, I have asked her every week, "How am I doing as a parent?" She is now nine and, as far as she is concerned, I am doing "Great." However, I know that this is going to change as she approaches her teenage years and wants more freedom and independence. But the purpose of this dialogue is not an ego boost for me. I know her love is there in the way she talks. The real purpose is to set the stage for later, when she can then freely express how she wants me to improve as a parent. By the way, she also asks, "How am I doing as a child?"

So, maybe you can initiate this with your family. Some parents will welcome this dialogue, but some are too insecure to receive help or direction from you. Remember, though, that this critiquing session is not meant to hurt anyone. It is meant to genuinely help one another.

Now comes the hardest question I have received from teenagers. "What if my parents just don't care about communicating with me or respecting what I have to say?" Or "What if they have said I was a mistake and they didn't really want me?"

Tough question, but in reality there's a very simple answer.

Crank up your level of appreciation. Whatever your parents do or don't do for you, if not for them, you wouldn't be here. They deserve a big thanks. Period.

If they aren't interested in building a better bond with you, focus your love elsewhere. There are many people who would love to have your appreciation. However, do your best to respect the position of your parents. The most functional societies, communities, and families are those where the elders are respected. However, I am a strong believer in elders acting respectably.

A small word of caution—we tend to become the type of person with whom we associate. Association is critical. Do your utmost to choose your friends wisely.

For the majority of you who genuinely can and want to improve your relationships with your parents, it all begins with understanding, appreciation, and respect. To enhance your understanding, walk a day in their shoes. To increase your appreciation, think what it would be like if that parent were forever removed from your life tomorrow. I will address the issue of respect a lot in the ensuing chapters, ranging from respecting yourself to respecting all of life's creatures.

In the end, no matter how frustrated or angry your parents may be sometimes, their role is one that most of them wouldn't change for the world. Nelson Mandela, who became president of South Africa in 1994 (after 27 years in prison for opposing the apartheid system) spoke eloquently on fatherhood when he said, "It is great to be the father of a nation, but it is better to be the father of a family—I missed that the most when I was in prison."

There are times when your family does slip down the priority scale, but almost every person standing over a casket regrets not having spent more time with that person. So don't hesitate to give your mom and/or dad a hug—no words are needed. They will understand.

"It never occurs to teenagers that someday they will know as little as their parents."

Teenager to parent: "Just stop telling me you understand me, okay? Because you don't. I'm different from other people! My problems are unique! Nobody knows what it feels like to be me but me!"

Parent to teen: "Everybody feels that way sometimes, honey."

Teen: "Not only don't you understand me, you don't understand that you don't understand me!"

From the comic strip *The Zits*

Chapter Three

Spirituality:
The Anchor for Your Journey

*U*SA *Weekend Magazine* (May 1998 issue) surveyed a broad section of teenagers in America. When asked what the two biggest influences in their lives were, the response was parents first and religion second. This survey is extremely encouraging, because one of the biggest downfalls of modern society has been the relegation of religion to the back burner of many people's lives. In most countries, religion was (and in some cases still is) what determined the law of how people lived their lives. What was even more significant in this survey was that 34 percent said religion played a "powerful role in their everyday lives." For those adults who are concerned about the direction that teenagers are taking, solace can be taken from this fact; it is a bright star in our somewhat challenging future. I would like to take the liberty of expanding the word religion to spirituality. Spirituality is the fountainhead of all religion. Religious discrimination has a strong tendency to cause wars. In fact, almost every war has included the aspect of religious conflict. Millions of gallons of blood have been spilled over religious denominational differences. However, in the six years I spent researching a book on leadership, I found that every great leader had a strong spiritual foundation. Without it, you are a boat without an anchor. If you don't educate your heart, you will have a lifetime of frustration. So much emphasis today is placed on material poverty, yet the biggest problem for most individuals (not just teenagers) is an immense spiritual poverty.

So that we're all on the same channel, we will work with the understanding that we are all spiritual beings. That is our permanence. Scientifically, we know that every seven years we get a completely new body. Our cells are changing every minute, and after a seven-year period, we will have a completely different body. In other words, the body does not contain a single one of the molecules that it contained seven years ago. So for those of you who are fourteen, you are beginning your third body that is housing your spiritual spark, your soul, or your life energy force. (In some ways, this chapter should be reversed with the chapter on understanding your parents, because we need to understand ourselves and who we are before we can truly understand others. However, I put the chapter on parents first because, for the majority of you, your relationship with your parents, whether good, bad, or marginal, seemed to be the number one topic.) The fact that one out of three of you in the United States sees religion as a powerful influence is very encouraging. Why? Because this will guide you more easily over the numerous hurdles of life. It will also help you search for a better understanding of life and who you are. Have you ever wondered why you are here? What is your purpose in life? Why did some of you get a female body and some of you a male body? Why do some of you have great family situations and others not so wonderful? Why are some of you so fearful of things and others so brave?

These are great questions for you to ask, and I encourage you to search for answers. Remember, one of the underlying themes in this book is that knowledge eliminates fear (and anxiety and frustration). Far too many people today are trying to meet the right person rather than be the right person.

You may hear your parents talking about investments (and some of you may even have investments yourselves). These are material investments. I can assure you that the best investment you will ever make in your life is the time spent improving who you are as a person—it's a spiritual investment. Your love, your care, your understanding, your thoughtfulness, your kindness, your perseverance—we will talk about some of these qualities as this letter unfolds, but for now we will view them as essential components in the makeup of you as a spiritual being.

So many teenagers today talk of being lonely. When you put it in perspective, this is incredible. Here we are in the most communication-intense era ever. We have so many toys of communication—phones, faxes, e-mails, the Internet—yet a large number of people talk about loneliness. The problem is we are so obsessed with these communication skills and tools that we are out of touch with ourselves. And if we don't know who we are and where we are going, we will feel a sense of uncertainty and ultimate isolation and loneliness.

When you think about it, if you work on yourself and become a really secure person, you will never be lonely. We should not fear solitude. Being alone allows us time to introspect—to look at ourselves.

Just as there is a sense of satisfaction in solving a puzzle or a math problem, there is an even greater sense of satisfaction and well being when we understand who we are and why we are here.

The majority of people believe in a Supreme Being or God in charge of the universe, but a small percentage believes we got these bodies by chance. This can easily be challenged by studying something as complex as an airplane or as simple as a table. Neither happened by chance. There was a designer or creator. So looking at this incredible machine called the human body, we should be in awe of it and deeply appreciate it. Who could create such an amazing "machine," where there is more activity going on in one cell than in the entire city of New York?

In order to be able to advance our spiritual life, we must conquer our minds. The mind is always active, even when we are asleep. That's why when someone asks what you are thinking and you say, "Nothing"—NICE TRY!

So how does one get peace of mind? When people talk about being peaceful and serene, what do they mean? This is where the Western world has a great deal to learn from the Eastern world. Some of you may have parents who are frightened or intimidated by anything that isn't familiar to them or that they don't understand. Words like yoga, meditation, reincarnation, transmigration, and mantras are uncharted waters for some people. Yet, understanding these spiritual terms and processes can be very beneficial.

And what about tai-chi, tae-kwon-do, karate, judo—the martial arts. Where do these fit into our society that is so entrenched in football, basketball, baseball, and hockey? They are all connected to the world of spirituality—spiritual discipline that will help us cope with an ever-increasingly turbulent, chaotic world.

If you are going to emotionally and mentally survive this world, you have to be like a duck. If you have ever watched a duck on the water, you'll see they look like they are calmly gliding through the water, yet underneath their feet are paddling like crazy. So even though you are physically part of a world that is moving very fast, your mind can be very calm because you understand who you are and why you are here. In the eye of the hurricane, it is very calm. Having a spiritual understanding allows us to be in that eye.

In visiting 134 countries, I have noticed there are three segments of the world population which seem to be quite calm. The first consists of those countries where the people understand they aren't in control of most events and accept the cards of life that are dealt to them. For example, about 80 percent of the men in America have back problems. Many American men try to control their lives and destiny. This is VERY stressful. On the other hand, back problems in the Middle East and India are almost non-existent. In the Middle East, the spiritual philosophy is *inshallah*: "It's God's will." Whatever happens, happens—Don't worry about it—Just accept it. In India, most people believe in the law of karma—that whatever comes their way, good or bad, is based on their activities in this lifetime or in past lives. They accept it and don't try to worry about it or control it.

The second group of people who are extremely peaceful are those who meditate. In simplified terms, meditation is the process of getting above the mind. One receives a mantra to chant. In Sanskrit (the original language of the world), "man" means mind and "tra" means above. Hence, while meditating on a mantra, you get above your mind and enter a peaceful state. (Your mind never turns off. It's not like your tape recorder which has an "off" or "pause" button.)

The third segment of calm individuals consists of those who live a simple life and have very minimal needs and wants. In most cases, they live in small towns and villages or on islands that haven't been bombarded with the world of advertisements. When you see something you want, your mind becomes agitated. You often get jealous or envious because you don't have it, or you become depressed because other people have things you don't have. This chasing of material goods for more and more enjoyment is not conducive for spiritual growth. On the other hand, there is nothing wrong with having material possessions—it just depends on what you use them for. Let's say you just turned 16 and got a new car. Are you using that car to drive around and impress people with your new toy? Or are you using the car to deliver food to the homeless or to drive to a local hospital where you are volunteering?

Throughout the rest of this book, this understanding of spirituality will be interwoven a lot. If you focus on your spiritual growth, you will be guaranteed a life that is full of satisfaction and happiness. If you doubt this, just spend time around some really wealthy people, and you will notice an absence of laughter, smiles, peaceful and happy faces, and fulfillment. They seem to have it all, but do they?

Thought for the day: There is an Indian belief that everyone is a house of four rooms - a physical, a mental, an emotional, and a spiritual room. Most of us tend to live in one room most of the time, but unless we go into every room every day, even if only to keep it aired, we are not complete.

Source: *House of Four Rooms* (Morrow)

"God comforts us not to make us comfortable, but rather comforters."

Chapter Four

Struggle and Adversity
(Your Real Teachers)

In many cultures, the early teenager's years are the time when real life education begins. In fact, it's really only been in the last hundred years and in countries like America that the life of a teenager has been so protected from the harsh lessons of adulthood. However, wounds can actually be a great source of wisdom.

So it's been interesting to see how many parents say that they don't want you to struggle like they did. They don't want you to face those hardships. As a result, they have made things a lot easier for you, and because of this, you have been deprived of one of the most educational experiences you will ever have. Some parents are so anxious to see their children have what they didn't have that they forget to give them what they did have.

Adversity and struggling are wonderful teachers. Life is always full of challenges. Adversity often introduces us to ourselves, and struggling makes us appreciate the end result so much more. Wally Amos, who became famous through his Famous Chocolate Chip Cookies, believes there are no negative experiences because, in his view, there's a lesson in every experience.

Every high school team has an athlete who is superbly talented, who can perform skills with very little effort or practice time. And each team has a player who has minimal talent, but works like crazy. When you have a situation where your team is losing in the last few seconds of a game, it is the guy who has paid the price in the trenches that you want on your side—the player who has fought hard and trained hard to earn the privilege to play. The naturally talented athlete has often had it too easy and will usually not respond well to crises or challenging moments in life. You seldom see millionaires' sons or daughters on an Olympic podium. Affluence usually undermines drive. They are externally filled up but are internally empty.

And then there are those of you who have never made it to any extra-curricular activity. You are usually in one of two groups. The first group of you are those who are too busy working, helping your family out. You may regret the missed chances to be part of these programs, but on the other hand, you are gaining valuable life lessons. Remember, we shouldn't reject or be upset over what we don't have, but should rather appreciate what we do have.

The second group of you are those who have parents who have spoiled you with presents or money, or have tried to win you over by showering you with material gifts. You always have money in your pocket, and you probably got a car the first day you were eligible to drive. You probably have the latest designer clothes and shoes. And your friends are probably envious of the opulent home you live in, with all the latest gadgets and toys. You are also in a group that has the highest suicide rate of any group (teenage or adult) in the world.

American teenagers, with all their rich, fancy surroundings, are very vulnerable to taking their lives. Why? How could this be? Here you are, the envy of so many kids in your school. Yet inside, most of you are hurting big-time. It's very simple to understand. You were deprived of the opportunity to earn that position on your own.

Personally, I feel the greatest disservice parents can do to their children is to not allow them the education of struggling. Children who get large inheritances are very often handicapped in their drive.

Many of you have ordered an ice cream at Baskin Robbins. What you probably don't know is that the company could have been owned by a young gentleman called John Robbins, son of founder Irv Robbins. John was offered the multi-million dollar business by his dad, but he turned it down because he felt that receiving so much money without working for it would ruin his integrity.

So many people's lives have been ruined by their receiving large sums of money from their parents at a young age. It's very similar to the lottery, where people win money that they didn't earn. And guess what they say about their lives a few years after winning? Almost all of them say their lives are worse. Winning all that money didn't make them happier. In fact, it put a lot more stress in their lives. They bought bigger toys. They bought more expensive toys. They bought toys they didn't even need but thought they should have as "rich people" now. They had people they didn't even know asking them for money. They worried about their new possessions getting stolen, and hence, their insurance bills skyrocketed.

As much as you would like to be handed a large sum of money, try hard to look at the bigger picture of life. Life is not about what you acquire, but rather what you give. A person who has everything materially is often a very poor person. Another valuable lesson is understanding that failure is not a crime. However, failure to learn from the failure or mistake, is. Every successful individual has a much longer list of failures than successes. Your character is always more tested by the defeats than by the victories. When you lose, don't lose the lesson.

As a TV interviewer for tennis, I've asked the winners and losers of tennis matches what they learned. The loser's answer is always much longer and much more thought-provoking than the winner's. Success can be a lousy teacher. However, when we lose, we have a terrific opportunity to learn.

I will talk about formal education in a later chapter, but it is an appropriate moment here to share with you my thoughts on exams. Even today when I hear the word exam, I shudder. The reason is that I was not a good student, and I came close to failing each exam. Fortunately, I had parents who didn't get upset when I got Cs and Ds, because they knew I had tried hard. This is the key—effort. Nobody should ever chastise you for not doing well, as long as you have tried hard. And how many of you have experienced your parents looking at your report card when you got 5 As and a B or a C, and they focused on the B or C and wanted to know what happened? Why didn't you get all As? Immediately, a brilliant effort is marred by a sense of failure. Or another common situation is where parents compare your report card with your brother's or sister's. As much as I respect a parent's position, I must say that this is irresponsible leadership.

A sense of failure often breeds insecurity. And insecurity leads almost everyone down the wrong path.

When you next see a funeral procession, you won't see a U-Haul behind that hearse. And if you were to check the pockets of the deceased, you can be pretty sure those pockets will be empty. Go to a hospital and watch a newborn baby come into this world. They don't even have pants on to put anything in.

All our material possessions are temporary. They are on loan. But our life's lessons are permanent. They go with us. And here is where I feel the Western world can really learn from the East. Before elaborating, let me ask you this question: Have you ever experienced a situation where you felt you had lived a previous life?

When polled today, about half of Americans believe they have lived before, and the other half believe they only have this one life. I'm one who believes that I've lived before. I've had too many "déjà vu" experiences to not believe this. These are situations where I felt I had been somewhere before, even though it was my first time in this lifetime. And looking back on my early childhood, I wonder where some of my fears came from. When I was three, I refused to cross a bridge on my tricycle. I was terrified of heights.

It wasn't until I was in my 20s that I could drive across a bridge without feeling that it was going to collapse as soon as I got on it. I'm sure all of you have had similar fears. And what about talent? How is it some kids at a young age have great voices and others do better by not opening their lips?

In most Eastern religions and spirituality, reincarnation is an integral part of the belief structure. The understanding is that they will either return to the "spiritual world," seen as their original home, or they will return to the material world to learn more lessons. For a moment, let's forget what your beliefs are and assume that you are all potentially going to return to this planet called Earth. Can you imagine how differently you are going to treat it? Have you ever been driving on a road behind people who throw their wrappers or cigarette butts out the window? Unless they are complete slobs, they wouldn't throw that stuff on their carpets, but they do it when driving, because they think they won't be by that area again. The American Indians had a great philosophy about doing things. They said you should look at your decisions and see what effect it will have seven generations from now.

Unfortunately, we have trouble seeing or caring how our decisions will affect things tomorrow. There are many really important lessons we can learn but, personally, I feel that if we could treat our families and all living entities on our earth with the respect and understanding that we were going to reconnect, then we would make some very different, very thoughtful decisions in our lives. Life is really about the choices you make, and as long as you live, you should try to learn how to live.

"The purpose of life is a life with a purpose."

"Grant that I may be given appropriate difficulties and sufferings on this journey so that my heart may be truly awakened and my practice of liberation and universal compassion may be truly fulfilled."

Tibetan prayer
Source: *Don't Sweat the Small Stuff*
by Richard Carlson

At ten minutes to seven on a dark, cool evening in Mexico City in 1968, John Stephen Akwari of Tanzania painfully hobbled into the Olympic Stadium—the last man to finish the marathon.

The winner had already been crowned and the victory ceremony was long finished. So the stadium was almost empty as Akwari—alone, his leg bloody and bandaged—struggled to circle the track to the finish line.

Dear Teenager

The respected documentary filmmaker, Bud Greenspan, watched from a distance. Then, intrigued, Bud walked over to Akwari and asked why he continued the grueling struggle to the finish line. The young man from Tanzania answered softly, "My country did not send me 9,000 miles to start the race; they sent me 9,000 miles to finish the race."

Story from *The Confidence Course*
by Walter Anderson

Chapter Five

We are All in Prison

When you think of a prison, you think of people behind bars, but that is a narrow, materialistic perspective, for in some aspect of life we are all in prison.

We can be prisoners of our fear, or our insecurities, or our financial status, our fame, or our addictions. Nobody is free. Yet today the passion for power, the greed for wealth, and the lust for fame seem to grow more and more.

Fame is an interesting one. So many people want to be recognized by others. Look at actors and actresses. They work very hard to finally get their names and faces into the bright lights. Yet as soon as they are famous, they hide behind their sunglasses, wigs, and big hats. They can't walk down the street without people wanting to talk to them or get their autographs. They can't eat quietly in a restaurant without people watching every move they make and trying to figure out the best time to come and talk to them. They become prisoners of their fame.

I remember one time driving on the Los Angeles freeway with Alan Alda, of the very successful TV series "M*A*S*H." It was around the time of the final episode, which would be seen by hundreds of millions of people around the world. I was amazed how many people honked and waved at him. Here we were on our way to play a game of tennis, and he couldn't even drive peacefully down the freeway. Up until that time, I had wanted to become famous.

As a teenager today, you have a huge challenge to get out of the prison of materialism. In this intensely materialistic era, you are constantly entreated to try to get more, buy more, and consume more material things. Advertising plays a major role in shaping your desires. Advertisements drive the engine of consumption. If you have younger brothers or sisters, or work in a store where young kids are shopping with their parents, you will notice the three favorite words of most kids. I WANT THAT. This is a recent phenomenon, largely brought on by the constant bombardment of visual images of new toys, foods, and games that flash in front of kids everywhere. As a teenager, your primary challenge is to avoid the pitfall that equates material possessions with happiness.

Another prison cell that is difficult for you to avoid getting locked into is the enormous pressure to smoke, drink, and do drugs. At this point, I will split the discussion into two parts. The first part is for those of you who haven't started any of these, and the second part is for those of you who have.

For those of you who are still free, it would be very helpful to reinforce your current status by visiting the alcoholic ward in a hospital, a drug rehabilitation center, or the lung cancer section of a hospital. Every time I hear that 3,000 kids will begin smoking each day in America, I just wish that prior to starting you would go to a hospital and see former smokers on oxygen ventilators, trying to get air into their badly scarred and damaged lungs. Or prior to beginning to drink, look at what you are about to do. It might help to understand what the word intoxication means. It's the fancy medical term for being drunk. If you extract part of the word—"toxic"—it means poison. Every time you consume an alcoholic drink, you poison or kill the cells in your body that the alcohol comes in contact with. So if the substances have such a negative effect on our bodies, why do people do it? The irony is that many teenagers do it simply because their parents or teachers have told them not to. In talking with your parents, it's almost as if the day you turn 13, you shift into a rebellious gear. Few teenagers make it through the teenage years without some sort of rebellion.

Yet doing something, regardless of your age, just because you shouldn't do it is simply part of our immaturity. Maturity means outgrowing the rebellious mentality. It is essential to note that I'm not against rebellion, particularly if it is against a blatant injustice. If you have a parent who is physically beating you all the time, you must rebel. But to begin smoking because your parents say "Don't" is simply the beginning step into the prison of eventual addiction.

Before doing anything, talk to people who are already where you want to go. Before smoking, talk to people who desperately want to quit but can't because they are addicted. Talk to people who are married to smokers but don't smoke themselves, and get them to tell you what the smoker's breath is like, and how their clothes, cars, and homes smell, and how the curtains are stained. Get a doctor to show you a picture of a smoker's lung, as well as the lung of someone who lives with a smoker.

Another reason teenagers begin smoking, drinking, or taking drugs is peer pressure. One of the most important chapters later on will be on self-esteem, insecurity, and self image. You end up doing things because you are worried about whether or not you will be accepted by your friends. So many adults are in the addiction prison today because they didn't have enough self-esteem and self-confidence as a teenager to be able to pass on the offer. One of the reasons people want to bring you into the world of negative habits is that they themselves are insecure. They want reinforcement. They are not content with themselves. They want you to participate. Remember, if they won't be your friends when you won't follow their lifestyle, you have learned a valuable lesson on friendship. Real friendship is not based on what you do, but rather on who you are as a person. One of the most destructive environments today is the alcohol prison. More families are fractured by alcohol than anything else. In fact, almost all domestic violence has an alcohol component.

How many parents have to bury their teenagers because of car accidents involving drunk drivers? A very high percentage of car accidents, overall, are alcohol related.

And what about the actual prisons? The *Los Angeles Times* reported recently that 80% of the 1.7 million people behind bars were involved in a crime where drugs or alcohol played a part. That's an incredible statistic. When under the influence of these substances, we often do things we would never do had we not taken them. We get out of control and lose our freedom.

Drugs and alcohol may help you cope for a few moments, but it doesn't help you deal effectively with things in the long-term. They are simply a band-aid solution.

Now, for those of you who have already started smoking, drinking, or doing drugs. You can read books, listen to lectures, and watch TV announcements telling you to stop, but in most cases, none of these will work until you understand yourself and what you are doing, and what you ultimately want to do, and why.

Most teenagers are under the illusion that when they start smoking, drinking, or doing drugs they are becoming free, or they can stop when they want. Understanding that something is taking control of your life might help alter this illusory thought process and motivate you to stop. Or understanding that you aren't respecting yourself by poisoning your body may help. Because we get this body for free, we often don't value it.

Being the captain of a sinking ship isn't always a glorious time. If you saw "Titanic," you witnessed the pain of the captain of the ship. Each day you show disrespect for your body, your ship sinks a little further.

This is the only part of the book I didn't want to write, because it deals with a choice that you've already made. Plus when you are young, you feel you will live forever, so talking about destroying your health really doesn't work. Also, you feel "cool" doing adult things you are not supposed to do. However, it might help to understand that just because your parents are making mistakes, it doesn't mean you have to follow them. In the end, self discipline is all that works, whether it's doing your homework, practicing free throws, throwing strikes, learning to play a musical instrument, or controlling your senses. You are the president of your body. If you care, you will make the changes. If you don't, you'll be forced to eventually change through ill health or accidents. Life is always better when you make the decision, rather than having it forced upon you.

Finally, what about the prison of fear? Everybody has fears—some more than others. What is interesting is that most of our fears never become realities. And it's also worth noting that the more simplified our existence, the less fear binds us. In a tiny village in Fiji where there are no cars on the island, the parents don't have to worry about their 16 year-old getting into a car accident or their toddler running into the streets and being run over.

One of the biggest ironies is that the United States of America is called "The Land of Freedom," yet it is a country of immense fear. Just look at how most of America locks itself in at night with deadbolts, chains, floodlights, burglar alarms, etc. It's great for those in the security business, but far too many people go to bed at night in fear. We are so "free" in America that we have imprisoned ourselves big-time.

There's a country in Asia called Singapore, which is perceived as a very strict country. They have a lot of laws. What is interesting is that there is an extremely low crime rate. People can safely walk the streets at any hour of the night. There's a sense of discipline throughout the country. Discipline to a teenager sometimes has a negative connotation. Yet you will have matured in life when you realize that freedom comes through both self-discipline AND discipline. The self-discipline to not smoke, drink, or do drugs frees you from something controlling you. The discipline to abide by the law keeps you out of prison. Self-discipline brings a freedom and peace to your life. The self-discipline to not always want something that someone on the TV ad beckons you to buy keeps you free from constantly having an agitated mind in search of more materialistic goods. To truly be free, you need a personal code of discipline. So the next time you hear about someone being in prison, look at yourself and see whether you can truly call yourself a free person.

"Where there's no self-discipline, there's no character."

Chapter Six

Don't Let School Interfere with Your Life Education

Your time spent in school has been a failure no matter how much it has done for you, unless it has opened your heart. Most of the current schooling system emphasizes book knowledge. An average of 14,500 hours are spent memorizing thousands of facts that you will never need again. It is not that this is all bad, because sometimes the process of learning, memorizing, and being disciplined will pay dividends later in life.

But there's a huge gap between students and teachers in schools today. The teachers say their two biggest concerns are your apathy and anger. And your two biggest concerns are that the classes are mostly boring and irrelevant. Wow! If this were a business relationship or a marriage, any outside advisor would bring the two parties together for discussion immediately! Let me share with you two suggestions that might help this situation immensely. First of all, look at how much time is spent training teachers how to be teachers. But virtually no time is spent teaching you how to be students. Sure, you were told to be quiet, pay attention, etc. But I'm not talking about the obvious stuff. I'm talking about how to listen, how to be of assistance to the teacher during the class so there is a connection. Learning begins with listening. Great teaching is effective communication between two people. The unfortunate thing today is that when most of you apply for a job, you haven't been taught outstanding listening skills, nor can many of you carry on a decent conversation for a long period of time. Articulating your thoughts and feelings is very difficult for many of you. I have personally interviewed over 10,000 people for positions with our company and discovered that less than five percent of the college graduates had reasonable communication skills. Each year I try to speak to 25 schools around the country, and I'm surprised how few students have good listening skills. My initial reaction was to blame you, but then I realized that nobody has trained you how to be good listeners. At the end, I used to allow 10-15 minutes for questions. Now I only leave 2-5 minutes, because there are so few questions. This is unfortunate, because the ability to ask questions is extremely valuable. It is through questioning that you learn. And the quality of your questions often determines the quality of your life. Oliver Wendell Holmes said it perfectly: "A mind stretched by new ideas never returns to its original state."

So what should be done for you? If I were commissioner of the educational system, I would suggest that the first two days of school be spent teaching you effective listening and communication skills and how to be a student. In another words, skills that will help the learning process for you.

Another idea I would implement would be a regular review by you, as students, of the teachers and the curriculum. What amazed me when I was in school was that I had a particular teacher three years in a row and he never got any better. His voice was a monotone all three years. Yet I later found out that his salary increased each year—just because he got older, not because he got better. And from what you've told me, things haven't changed.

In talking with teenagers extensively over the last couple of years in preparation for writing this book, I found your assessment and evaluation of your teachers to be extremely thoughtful and perceptive. It wasn't a gripe session—it was an honest evaluation. The good teachers got rave reviews from you, and the bad ones got lots of suggestions on how to improve. The unfortunate thing is that these evaluations never got to the teachers. The system doesn't allow it.

Right now, a teacher gets evaluated by the principal or a senior educator during a short period of time. I'm sure none of you missed how some of your teachers changed when an evaluator was present. The evaluator sits in and watches for a couple of hours, if that. But you are there every day—your evaluation is much more valuable.

As far as what is being taught, you should have some input. Obviously, there are areas of no compromise, information that is essential. However, the world is changing, and you can give some very valuable input. In addition, the fact that you have some say in what is taught means that you would be much more receptive in receiving it from your teachers.

Most of us don't remember what we've been taught, but we usually remember who the outstanding teachers were. In one of the seminars I give for corporations, I ask people to list the teacher(s) who had the greatest impact on them when they were teenagers. Most could only remember one, some remembered two teachers. They remember their names and the qualities that made them a great teacher. They don't remember what material they were taught, and in some cases, they even forgot the subject. But they do remember the life's education they got from that person.

Formal education, as you know it, is only a couple of hundred years old. People used to learn about life from their parents and people in the village, mostly the senior people, and mostly by storytelling. Stories were (and still really are) the heart and soul of communication. Long before the construction of libraries, stories were the primary means of learning. They also helped convey lessons learned through practical application. Recently, many schools have begun requiring that you put in a certain number of hours of community service in order to be able to graduate. This is fantastic, because it connects you to the real world. You may not enjoy this at times, but in the long run you will look back on it as one of the best learning experiences. Most of all, it stops you momentarily from focusing on yourself, and anytime you can do this, your learning curve increases. I feel this is a wonderful idea and have been disappointed with psychologists and human rights people who criticize it as an abuse of the student's time.

We are born with a deep core of creativity, and modern schooling inhibits that in a great many instances. Exams, for example, inhibit creativity because we don't want to fail. Yet the great inventors and artists fail all the time. As well, we need to create an environment where we can understand things. One of the problems with the computer, for example, is that you can access information but you may not understand it. There is no question that reliance on a computer to do the actual work leads to a lack of original thinking and writing skills. We've gone from the rhythms of nature to the rhythms of the electronic age.

Can you imagine how different your day in school would be if you were able to help in designing the curriculum? If you were able to help the teachers be better teachers, and if you really understood how to be a better participant in the learning process? Maybe you want to have your principal read this chapter.

There's one final concern of the teachers that we haven't addressed yet, and that is the concern about the anger of the students. I will address this further in the chapter on health, but let's talk a little bit about why people get angry. A lot of blame is placed on TV and movies, and justifiably so. TV and movies are filled with so many violent acts, like murder and assault, that they are made to seem like everyday events. And the media glorifies violence, thereby desensitizing you to it. The reason people are able to pull the trigger so easily is that they have learned to shut down their empathetic response.

Yet how do you account for the fact that some people will watch a violent movie and come out calm and unaffected, while a few may come out more angry?

The anger is the result of deep-seated frustration. And frustration in teenagers is often a result of two things: not being able to truly express your feelings and make a difference, and also just not understanding the situation. When we are young, we tend to find fault with what we don't understand. Actually, some adults are like that, so maybe we should change the word young to immature. I've met some very mature young people and very immature old people.

The 1990s saw the ushering in of metal detectors in schools because of guns and knives being brought there. I cannot imagine what some of you who first walked through the metal detector when entering school must have felt. We've come to expect terrorism in the global adult world, but in schools? In 1997-99 we saw a number of children gunned down by their classmates. After the Columbine High School shooting in Colorado, the phone rang off the hook at Garrett Metal Detectors in Garland, Texas. Schools are now big customers. Another reaction is to add police on and around the school grounds. We talked about prisons earlier. Do you start to feel like your schools are moving toward a prison-like atmosphere?

So how does one deal with a frustrated student? Very often, communication is helpful. Participation and helping to change alleviates further frustration. And I hope you will all read the chapter on health.

What we eat may be one of the most important influences in helping to regulate our emotions. This is an area virtually nobody has talked about. Sure, there will always be the occasional student who will major in trouble, but there needn't be so many who are frustrated. You may have heard your parents say that REAL EDUCATION begins the day you finish school. There's lots of truth in that. The real education gained while in school, however, is actually understanding the process of learning, asking questions, communicating, and interacting. It's not memorizing how many presidents of the U.S. there have been or who wrote the book *Lost Horizon* that is really important, but rather it is the experience of this journey that is your true education.

"You go or grow through an experience."

"Any new high school student who doesn't understand that he or she is about to enter adulthood on the cusp of the most tumultuous changes in human history has been abused by the school."

World Watch, May/June 1999

Chapter Seven

Are You a Victim or a Victor?

When you get up in the morning, you really only have one major decision to make, and that is whether you are going to have a good attitude or a bad attitude. Deciding on what clothes to wear or how to do you hair is minor compared to this one critical decision that will always determine how your day will turn out.

For those of you who have watched some of the daytime talk shows where people spew out their troubled lives to the world (even people in small towns in Saudi Arabia watch them now), you may have noticed one common denominator. Almost every one of these troubled people places the blame elsewhere for what has gone wrong. They blame parents, kids, brothers, sisters, relatives, friends, teachers, bosses, employees, school, society, the world. It's incredible how many people say the system failed them. People are responsible for their actions. Systems aren't responsible for actions.

This lack of taking responsibility is borne out in American prisons. Almost all the prisoners I've talked to in America say they don't belong there. It's some-one else's fault that they are behind bars. What is it about our society that causes us to refuse to accept responsibility for our actions? Why are we only the victims?

America has the most mental institutions of any country in the world. We are near the top in cases of depression per capita. We consume billions of dollars worth of anti-depressant drugs. Why do we have so much trouble dealing with what comes our way?

It basically comes down to our inability to accept or understand that we are the pillars of our destiny. We have to stop blaming other people. You really won't have opportunities without accepting responsibility. It's very dangerous to nurture "victim consciousness." All of you have classmates or friends whose home sit-uations are quite different from one another. There's the kid who has only one parent and that parent is working two jobs to put food on the table, put clothes on the kid's back, and provide a place to rest their heads at night. The kid doesn't have much time to play or go to the mall or to the movies, because there are two younger siblings to help care for. Yet this kid gets great grades and is someone whom you would love to get to know more and be around. The kid doesn't complain, is always smiling, and appreciates life. Then there is the kid whose parents are wealthy. The family is healthy. The kid has boodles of time to hang out at the local mall and a large allowance to buy things. The kid is always complaining about people and life and his overall attitude is well below par. Criticizing teachers, parents, and friends is this kid's modus operandi.

In spite of their opposite situations, both are potential victims. The first kid has lots of hardships, and the second has a life that is too easy. One chooses a positive approach, the other a negative one.

But the real difference is that the first kid chooses not to be a victim. He chooses to be the victor. You may have learned responsibility as a young child. If so, full credit to your parents. In fact, let them know how much you appreciate them instilling that in you. If you haven't learned it yet, then I would highly recommend you place it near the top (if not at the very top) of things to work on. Responsibility almost always leads to self-respect.

What does it actually mean to be responsible? In simple terms, it means that you will honor your word, and that you accept what comes your way and deal with it accordingly. If you have a midnight curfew and you get back at 12:15 a.m. and you are grounded, don't yell at your parents. There are no excuses. In the business world you might lose your job for being late; at home you just lose a few extra hours of freedom.

You may have noticed that throughout a major portion of this book, I have sympathized with a lot of what you, as teenagers, are dealing with. But here's where I'll be totally, 100 percent on the side of your parents. If you messed up, apologize, accept the penalty, and respect the situation. Lesson learned. Period.

Being responsible means honoring your commitment to whatever you do, not just being on time. It means understanding how your actions (or inaction) affect those around you as well.

In life you represent three things: 1) yourself; 2) your family; and 3) a variable—your school, your team, your company, your country, etc. If you are responsible, you do your best to represent these three well at all times. And you will do it without carrying extra baggage.

Let's say you are a member of your high school basketball team. The night before a big game, your father consumed an excess amount of alcohol, lost control, and physically abused you. You are classified in the law book as a victim. You can nurture that consciousness and physically assault a teammate, and then blame your poor performance in the game and the way you treated your teammates on your father's actions the night before. Or you can choose to break the circle of violence. You can choose to be responsible. How many times do you see these "victims" on TV talking about how they were abused as a child and twenty years later they still can't take responsibility for their actions?

Every person wakes up every day with something wrong, whether it be physical, mental, emotional, or psychological. Nobody is free from this. Every one of the 5.6 billion people on this planet is in the same situation. But if we want to be truly free, we must stop being fearful and accept responsibility. A courageous person dies a single death, but a fearful person dies a thousand. We must be courageous enough to accept the fact that we must pay for our indiscretions.

I'm sure you've all seen situations where someone is caught on video committing a crime. Then, the next day they say before the judge, "Not guilty." What signal does that send to you as teenagers? I feel badly that you have to be exposed to that kind of irresponsibility. I'm sorry that you read about an NBA basketball player punching a coach, then being fired, and then suing for being fired.

This player was given the opportunity to play basketball. With that opportunity comes freedom. And with that freedom comes responsibility—responsibility to act within a certain frame of guidelines. He is free to punch his coach—nobody challenges that. But with that action comes a reaction. Responsible people accept it and move on. Irresponsible people once again claim they have been harmed.

As a teenager you are longing to be treated as an adult. I can tell you that accepting responsibility in a mature manner is probably the fastest ticket to the adult world.

In continuing to accept it throughout your life, you will definitely alter the altitude at which you fly. When you make mistakes, do your very best to accept the consequences. I'm sure many of you have experienced your parents' reaction.

When you've made a mistake, were extremely repentant, accepted the consequences, and didn't blame anyone but yourself, how did your parents react? Quite differently from when you denied it was your fault and yelled at them, saying they are "terrible, unfair parents."

Most people don't like disciplining others. It's hard work. Ask your teachers, ask your parents, ask managers at jobs. Almost everybody would prefer that you discipline yourself. This is true responsibility. If you back your parents' car into a post, immediately take charge. Promise you will pay for the repairs. You will honor that commitment. You were driving. You were responsible. If you were expelled from school for misbehaving or for some indiscretionary act, then write the principal of the school and whoever else was involved an apology letter. One to your parents would help big-time as well. Remember, they took the responsibility of raising you, and part of them was expelled, too. It may be embarrassing to face a situation, but learning to place the blame on your own shoulders—no one else's—will strengthen you for the rest of your life.

It's not necessarily the mistakes that affect you long-term; it's usually your reaction to the mistakes that ruins you. The greatest freedom you have is to change your attitude. And remember that the life you are born into is not necessarily your destiny. You really do have the opportunity to rewrite your story.

> "We cannot direct the wind, but we can adjust the sails."

Chapter Eight

Can You Really Be Happy?

When I asked teenagers what the purpose of life is, the majority of you answered, "To be happy." Fair enough. This is an answer that lots of people, regardless of age, give. The second question was "What makes you happy?" Guess what the common thread was throughout your answers? It was materialistic possessions, things that can be destroyed in a few seconds, that you thought made you happy. Shopping, nice house, nice cars, good-looking boyfriends, good-looking girlfriends, money, etc. Very, very few of you mentioned anything to do with happiness coming from what you do for others. Yet happiness really does belong to those who live to serve others. The older you get, the more you realize that kindness is synonymous with happiness. Only by helping others can we achieve true happiness and balance in our lives. And best of all, when you serve others, you will never be out of a job.

As mentioned earlier, advertising forces us to focus mostly on the concept that if we get some "thing" we will be happier. Yet we burn out quickly on material things. Remember that CD that you bought that you couldn't wait to listen to? You played it 10-15 times the first day, thinking you would never tire of it. Yet a week later, the level of enjoying it was nowhere near what it was the first day. Once we get the object we struggled so hard for, there's a flash of joy, but the next moment we are unhappy again. Trying to satisfy ourselves materially is impossible. Anyone who has eaten too much on Thanksgiving or Christmas Day can attest to the fact that there's a limit to how much we can eat. Similarly, as we expand our list of desires, we move further into a realm of dissatisfaction. The desire to have more and more is insatiable.

However, when it comes to giving our service to others, there are no limitations. And your greatest reward is not in what you get back for yourself, but rather what you become in the process. Also, giving and serving helps us see beyond our selfish desires and egocentric concerns. And your ability to give has nothing to do with your financial status. In September of 1997, two of the most revered people of this century left us. Princess Diana was wealthy, beautiful, famous, and powerful. She was called the most photographed woman ever. The other, Mother Teresa, died with her sari-like outfit and sandals as her only possessions. What caused such respect and outpouring of emotion when these two left us was the fact that they both served in a humble manner. Both were troubled with an inner passion about the injustices in life and yearned to help out those who were less fortunate. A *USA Weekend* article on teenagers (May 1, 1998) said that 70 percent of teenagers surveyed experienced depression. That's a huge percentage, considering that this is a time in your life when most of you aren't burdened with responsibilities or providing a livelihood for your family, holding onto a job, raising children, or worrying about putting enough money away for your retirement.

Time for a suggestion. The next time you're feeling sorry for yourself or depressed, visit the cancer ward of a young children's hospital. You will see kids who only have a few weeks or months left to live, yet so many are full of life and smiles. No matter how bad your situation is, there are many others who are in far worse shape than you are. When I was a teenager, I was a fussy eater. That changed significantly after I went on the professional tennis tour. One of my first stops was Bombay, India. I got up very early one morning to practice, and there was a truck driving by with a guy shoveling dead bodies into the back of the truck. These were people whose home was the street, and they had died that night of starvation. The night before in the hotel, I hadn't finished my dinner. These people would have given anything to have had my leftovers. Since that experience, I've seldom not cleaned my plate.

When we volunteer our time without expectation of anything in return, there's a wonderful feeling. Almost everyone you meet is carrying a heavy burden, and by being kind and giving to them, something exciting happens. By making others the center of your attention, your anxieties, worries, and fears start going away. Happiness is also found during times of pure simplicity. Today we're running around like a bunch of rats in the day to day cage of life. We don't take time to watch a sunset or just enjoy the sound of the birds. We're always wondering or thinking about what we're going to do next. We live in an era of 6 to 8 second visual and sound bytes, and it doesn't make us happy.

Another thing to understand about happiness is that it is almost entirely dependent on your attitude, not your circumstances. We all know people who have had a relatively easy life and yet are quite unhappy, and we know individuals who have suffered a lot and yet are very happy. The happiest people don't always have the best of everything—BUT they make the best of what they have. Another challenge for you is that you are growing up in an era of illusion. When two people are falling in love in a movie, there is music in the background, the lighting is perfect, the actors and actresses are handsome and beautiful. Makeup covers any blemishes. Reality isn't like that.

There are a great many books, even for the very young, that imply that someone "lived happily ever after." NOBODY in this material world lives happily ever after. The hard knocks of reality prevent this illusive, blissful state.

Some of you have commented that you don't feel that you have anything to give. It's natural to feel that way, particularly if you don't have a lot of confidence. However, if you think like that, you aren't giving yourself enough credit. Let me tell you one thing that you can contribute right away. Most of you can read and talk. Do you know how many people are lying in hospital beds today without enough strength to hold a book or open their eyes? Yet they are fully conscious. And for you to read or talk to them would make a huge difference. It would bring a ray of sunshine into their lives. By focusing on others, happiness naturally winds its way into your existence. TO THE WORLD YOU MAY BE ONE PERSON, BUT TO ONE PERSON YOU MAY BE THE WORLD.

As I have traveled the world, I have been amazed how much happier people are in simple settings. For some reason, the more we get, the more we want. It took me a long while to understand that contentment in life lies not in great wealth but in simple wants.

Another thing that might be helpful for you is to realize that happiness is not an object to go after. And you never know when that feeling of happiness will land in your heart. What seems to be evident is that happiness is a by-product of our efforts to help and serve others. However, even in our service, happiness will not be permanent. This is a world of duality. Just as there is hot and cold, there is happiness and sadness. Even the happiest people in the world aren't always happy.

I always remember the intense feelings I experienced at the beginning and end of summer as a young kid. The day after school finished, we headed to a cottage for two months. There I was, ecstatic—no school for two months. And the last day of summer stands out as one of deep sadness. I never wanted the sun to set that day. It was too good—too much fun. I wanted it to stay light forever.

Today as soon as people experience sadness, they try to cover it up with alcohol or drugs. Earlier, in the chapter on adversity, I mentioned that times of challenge help us to grow. And periods of sadness are opportunities for us to face the situation head on rather than cover it up. There are two key ingredients in life. The first is to grow, and the second is to contribute in a meaningful way. By growing, we gain self-confidence. By contributing, we feel good. And both self-confidence and feeling good about our service to others enable us to be much happier. Those having the emotional intelligence and the ability to tune into other's needs have a far superior chance of experiencing a better life.

In the 1960s former President John F. Kennedy instituted the Peace Corps. This is a group of mostly young, adventurous people who go to other countries to help out in local towns, villages, and communities. When these people returned for debriefing after their overseas assignment of a few years, almost all of them said that they gained more than they had given. It's an interesting phenomenon. The next time you're feeling depressed, quickly jot down what is making you depressed. You will see that most of the reasons are focused on something you don't have. This is our nature. And it leads to envy, another negative dart in your consciousness. We are envious that our neighbors have something we don't have. Because of this mentality, we live in one of the most dissatisfied cultures on record.

So instead of making happiness your goal, replace it with a sincere effort to concentrate on others, no matter how tough your situation is. You will be surprised how happiness will become more and more a part of your life. One final thought: A great many people try to find happiness in their memories. In fact, memories are often called a second chance at happiness. Still others focus on the future in hopes of finding happiness. The following quotes say it all about finding happiness in the present.

I Was Dying.

First I was dying to finish high school and start college.

And then I was dying to finish college and start working.

And then I was dying to marry and have children.

And then I was dying for my children to grow old enough for school so I could return to work.

And then I was dying to retire.

And now I am dying—and suddenly I realize I forgot to live.

—*Chinese proverb*: "If you want to find happiness for one hour, take a nap. If you want to find happiness for one day, go to the forest or the beach. If you want to find happiness for one month, get married, and if you want to find happiness forever, serve others."

"Harmony leads to happiness and happiness leads to harmony."

"I don't want a long funeral. And if you get somebody to deliver the eulogy, tell them not to talk too long. Tell them not to mention that I have a Nobel Peace Prize. Tell them not to mention that I have 300 or 400 other awards. I'd like someone to mention that day that Martin Luther King, Jr. tried to give his life serving others."

Martin Luther King

Chapter Nine

Through the Looking Glass

For some reason, teenagers, particularly in the Western world, experience a drastic plunge in self-worth between the age of 13 and 17. This is dangerous, because the moment we lose self-esteem, we suffer from depression, an inferiority complex, and negative thinking. Of all the challenges you face as a teenager, I personally see this as one of the important factors as to whether or not you will enjoy your teenage years. As a young child, you were full of hope, ideas, and dreams. Then something happens at about twelve or thirteen. You start to doubt yourself and see all kinds of obstacles in your path. If you have younger brothers and sisters from about five to nine years of age, you will see that they are quite positive in what they are going to accomplish with their lives. But talk to many teenagers about their future and the responses border mostly on the negative. A major reason for this is that you have been gradually transferring from the world of fantasy to the world of reality: it's a time when we begin filling our heads with limitations that prevent us from trying.

I have a really hard time with the concept of Santa Claus. We make him into a real person for young kids. Yet, they see a different Santa on a different street corner in a different mall and on different TVs, all within a few hours. There comes a time when parents have to say to their kids that there really isn't a person called Santa Claus per se, but the spirit of Santa Claus will always live. In spite of the difficulties that I personally have with the concept, the last Christmas card that I sent to my dad before he passed away had the words in it, "I will never say believing in Santa is wrong. Back when I was a kid, I lived in a house with him all year long."

I also have a problem with the tooth fairy and the Easter bunny. Our parents are simply trying to give us a happy childhood. But did their good intentions set us up to wonder what else we're going to find out isn't real?

When you were young and you told your parents what you wanted to be when you grew up, it didn't matter what you said—they patronized you and said you can become whatever you want. Then, when you moved into your teenage years, if you wanted to have a job or a career in something they didn't like, a conflict often arose.

Or heaven forbid if you haven't decided what career path you will follow by the time you are 13. And what about the parents who already have a script for your entire life? Or the parents who approve or disapprove of your career based on how much money you will make? The odds of children having exactly the careers that parents have mentally chosen for them are so minuscule that if parents could set aside this discussion, a huge area of conflict would be eliminated. Besides, parents should focus on their kids becoming good people first. Whatever job they have later won't be that relevant if they have a solid, good attitude. In fact, there are so few people coming into the job market with a positive, enthusiastic attitude that those who do can pretty much choose what they want to do.

Your self doubts as a teenager range over everything from looks to your relationships with adults. You are experiencing major changes in many facets of your life. The reality of life is setting in. You have requested more independence, and with independence come responsibilities. With responsibility come choices, with choices come mistakes. With mistakes comes the potential to lose your self-confidence.

Self-confidence has almost always been the secret to success. Not self-centeredness. Not being egotistical. But believing in yourself. If you watched Michael Jordan play basketball, you'd know he could miss seven shots in a row and yet never hesitate to try number eight with two seconds remaining. Great athletes and other successful people have the ability to learn from their mistakes and not dwell on them. You have to accept the fact that you are going to make many mistakes in your life and that you will be a basket case if they monopolize your thoughts. In fact, if you aren't careful, you become a prisoner of your weakness. But just as negative thoughts and dwelling on your weaknesses can hurt you, so can over-confidence hurt you.

Today, the athletic world is full of players who are into self-promotion. Look at the players who cross the goal line in NFL football and then proceed to do a dance for the crowd. This is pure self-celebration and demonstrates a very insecure person. The player got across the goal line because ten other players worked very hard in clearing the way for him. First and foremost, he should go and thank each of the ten players for helping him out. Instead of showing off, secure players will drop the ball. It's no big deal—they have the self-confidence to know that they will be back across the goal line again soon.

Whenever you encounter a person who is boasting or bragging, you can understand that this is a very insecure person. Insecure people are desperately trying to draw attention to themselves. This is why you see so many teenagers today sporting tattoos and a rainbow of hair colors and different attires. When people aren't comfortable with who they are, they work very hard to get people to notice them. In many ways they are hurting inside and crying out for recognition because their self-esteem has plummeted so much.

It takes courage to admit that you're insecure as a teenager. This may be perceived as vulnerability. And the last thing you, as a teenager, want to show to an adult (or even your peers) is any indication that you might be vulnerable. This is why you have trouble saying "no" to your peers when they want you to do something indescretionary. If you say, "I'm not comfortable with that," or "I'd rather not," you suddenly feel very vulnerable—vulnerable to ridicule from your peers. So instead of standing strong and being secure in your feelings, you give in, and another conflict begins inside of you.

Another example is swearing. Have you noticed that those friends of yours who swear the most are almost always the ones with the least amount of self-confidence? Or even in your own life, when you find things spinning out of control, you may swear more. When I was 25, I read that swearing shows people how insecure you are. It is said to be the effort of a feeble mind to express itself forcibly.

In the last chapter, I emphasized the importance of focusing on the present in order to experience a stronger and more prolific arena of happiness. However, it is valuable to spend some time in the future as well. Dreaming is important. Dreams are the blueprints of your ultimate achievements. Nothing happens without first being a dream. If you talk to people who are successful, you will find they were successful in their minds before they were successful in reality. Seeing a dream become a reality is huge for your confidence.

When talking about self-confidence, we need to realize that an important key to being secure about what you can do is preparation. Preparation gives you confidence, and the quality of your preparation determines your outcome. When giving a speech in school, for example, it is only the rarest of individuals who can stand up and present an enlivening, thoughtful, and entertaining subject without preparation.

We spend a lot of time in school preparing for presentations to our teachers and our coaches and our classmates. Yet we spend virtually no time on developing ourselves as individuals. If we are secure in who we are, without decorating our bodies or communicating in a self-absorbed manner, then life is so much easier.

If you mentally go through the people in your life who are the pillars to whom you go in crises, you'll find

that often they are the people who "have it together."
Another bonus of having it together is that people
with such self-esteem are seldom violent or mean people. As well, they are inclined to have good value
structures. They are also less fearful. It is just like a
good soldier going to do battle. If he is well prepared
and believes in his abilities, his fear will be minimized.

I wasn't sure whether to place the subject of
teenage sex in this book, and if so, whether it should
be under the section of addictions or self-esteem. I
chose the latter, since teenage sex is so often related to
self-respect. Your body is your temple. You can share
your thoughts, your feelings, and your friendship, but
you don't have to share your body. The biggest challenge that many of you face is that you make decisions
on the spur of the moment. It will really help if you
can make the decisions and choices ahead of time.
This way you'll have a clear vision when you are confronted with the situation. Your game plan has been
formed.

Many of you fold to the temptations because you
didn't think about the situation in advance. Whether
it is alcohol, smoking, drugs, or sex, do your best to
prepare for the time when your friends want you to do
something that may cause you a lifetime of regret,
addiction, or heartache.

Self-esteem includes the ability to recognize your attributes and being able to admit your faults. Knowing your strengths gives you confidence. And confidence allows you to have the desire and courage to confront your weaknesses. Without self-confidence, your self-image continues to plummet, and even your good qualities are camouflaged.

I will leave you with Eleanor Roosevelt's famous quote, which has helped so many people:

"Nobody can make you feel inferior without your permission."

Eleanor Roosevelt

"When I was fifteen and beat a rival to the basket, the frustrated teen spat on me. I disarmed him with grace. He didn't know what to do. I didn't respond the way he thought I would by hitting him or spitting. I retaliated by winning the game."

Magic Johnson
(former NBA basketball player)

"The way to feel better about yourself is to make others feel better."

Chapter Ten

Is Life Worth Living?

Is life worth living? You bet it is! But before we talk about why life is worth living, we need to look at some amazing statistics. I'm not someone who likes to write about or dwell upon statistics. However, the following will help you understand why I am devoting an entire chapter to this topic.

Some Statistics in the U.S.

1. 1,000 kids per day in the U.S. attempt suicide.
2. Suicide is the number 3 cause of death for individuals between 15 - 24.
3. Suicides tripled from 1950 to 1980, and then tripled again from 1980 to 1990.
4. 37 percent of teenagers have friends who have talked about or tried to commit suicide.

5. More people die from suicides then homicides
   each year.

(Source: Center For Disease Control)

What is it that causes you to want to end your life shortly after it is getting under way? There are hundreds of books, articles, and theories discussing the reasons, but there seem to be two common elements present in people who consider, attempt, or successfully commit suicide. First, these individuals do not understand the real purpose of life, and secondly, they have slipped into a selfish mode. Alan Loy McGinnis, in his book called *Confidence: How to Succeed at Being Yourself*, relates a wonderful story about an individual who contemplated suicide and went on to become world famous:

"Standing on the windswept shores of Lake Michigan one wintry night, ready to throw himself into the freezing waters, a 32-year-old bankrupt dropout happened to gaze up at the starry heavens. Suddenly he felt a rush of awe, and a thought flashed through his mind: *You have no right to eliminate yourself. You do not belong to you. You belong to the Universe.*

R. Buckminster Fuller turned his back to the lake and began a remarkable career. Best known as the inventor of the Geodesic Dome, by the time of his death, he held more than 170 patents and was world famous as an engineer, mathematician, architect, and poet."

Buckminster Fuller's story is very typical of those who have thought about or attempted suicide and lived. One hundred percent of those I've talked to who had been in the position of potentially killing themselves were grateful to be alive today. Many were surprised how fleeting the thought of suicide was in terms of the big picture of life.

There's a sunrise every day. It's always beautiful above the clouds, no matter how stormy your day is. Not every day is going to be full of sunshine for you. There will be challenging days, challenging situations, and challenging people. And it is here where we can tie together some of the previous chapters.

One of the keys to life is accepting the challenges. Climbing a mountain requires a lot more work than sliding down it. I talked earlier about struggling and how beneficial the process was. If you don't climb the mountain, you don't appreciate the view.

It's interesting to note that suicides are increasing in the more affluent segments of societies. In America the most disadvantaged group are elderly, impoverished black people. Yet they have the lowest suicide rate. As countries become wealthier and more developed, their suicide rates go up. In poorer countries, teenagers are depended upon by their parents as a form of security for unemployment, illness, and old age. Teenagers are regarded as economic assets as they become major contributors to the families by cooking, cleaning, working the fields, fetching water and firewood, etc. They are so focused on helping out the family that they don't have time to worry about themselves. In wealthier countries today, parents tend to let their children travel the easier route. And the easier route usually doesn't build character—character that will help one transcend emotional and mental crises.

When you have a "desert" experience, you don't want to remain stranded in the desert. In other words, if you are feeling low, develop a plan of action to get yourself out of the desert. We are pilgrims on the same journey. Those that keep going just have a better map. In addition, some journeys in life are longer and harder than others. If you can't do it alone, find a guide, like the sailor who uses the stars as a guide.

It is also worth noting that in times of crisis, like wars and natural disasters, suicides go way down. The reason is that people are so focused on caring for others along with their own struggle for survival that they don't have time to be in a state of depression. Psychiatrists and psychologists can write zillions of books and appear on TV night after night with ideas, suggestions, and plans of action regarding how to lower suicide rates. However, until the emphasis of life is on the understanding of service, suicides will go up.

I totally disagree with suicide and will never support you doing it. However, I do understand why you feel such despair. Many of you come home to neighborhoods that are no longer safe. Many of you come home to an empty house after school. You turn on a TV and see people fighting one another on talk shows. You see violence on every second channel. You become desensitized to others' pain. You look at your heroes, the athletes, and hear on the news that they have been arrested for drunk driving or possession of drugs. 2.4 million of you have a parent in jail. You hear about your political leaders cheating. You read about business people making immoral millions. You learn about all the chemicals that are poured into your food, the land, the water, and the air. You see your friends reveling in cheating.

I don't know how you felt after reading this last paragraph but, even though I'm a very positive person, I felt a sense of sadness writing it.

You might ask what gets me through. It's very simple. I continually try to devise a plan of action to give me peace of mind. For instance, you probably sense that I am tired of the pompous attitudes of most professional athletes. Sure, we have a few who are great at their sport and do maintain a sense of humility. Even though I'm a former professional athlete, I just don't watch sports on TV anymore. That's why I don't get agitated. Tough call? Not really. The time I spent watching sports has been replaced with time for my family or time to be of service to others.

What about the chemicals and the devastation of our land due to our poor food choices? Instead of complaining and getting depressed, I have chosen to write about it and do seminars on the subject to help make people aware.

Speaking of sporting events, have you ever been at one where spectators all around you are yelling at players and telling them how to do better? Most of these guys would have trouble running around the block without gasping for air, and here they are playing expert in the security of their seats. This is what many of you may be doing in this thing called life. It's human nature to sit on the sidelines and be critical of those who are in the arena. On the island of Jamaica there is a saying that there are two types of people. One group plants trees and the others come to sit under the planted trees.

I remember coaching a group of junior tennis players from age 14-18 in Hawaii, where I live. As part of the conditions for staying in this basically free program, they had to coach a group of youngsters from 10-13 in team tennis. As soon as this was implemented, they became far superior students. What happened? They had become teachers and realized how hard teaching was. They walked in the teacher's shoes. I know of some schools that have done this. Every week a student teaches a class. They find out how tough it is, and their respect for teaching and their teachers grows dramatically.

Sometimes you, as teenagers, look at this confusing world that adults have created and wonder how can you make a difference. Simply by caring enough to change the inside of you, you can change the world outside you. It's a chance to become a better pilot of your life and help those around you.

With every opportunity you usually have two options. Let's say you were handed a bag of cement and water. You could build a wall around yourself, or you could build stepping stones to and from yourself.

Letting others into your life is wonderful therapy. This is why the suicide phone line has been so successful. Just talking things out allows people a chance to explain what was depressing them. In addition, time heals. Look at your emotional mood swings. One minute you can be happy, the next minute you can be sad. This is why everybody who survives a suicide attempt is so thankful. Things do get better. But it's tough to do it without some help. Very few people come out of suicidal tendencies by themselves.

The following analogy may help you realize that the burden of life is lightened when we get some assistance. If you have 100 pounds of rocks and a boat to carry them in, the rocks won't sink. But if you don't have a boat, even a small pebble will sink to the bottom.

No matter what culture you're in, what age group, whether male or female, people rise to the occasion to help others in need. A person who is contemplating suicide is in need big-time. Just give others a chance first. Chances are you will be around a long time to return the favor.

"Only if you've been in the deepest valley can you enjoy the view from the highest mountain."

"You can't control the world around you, but you are the master of your soul."

Chapter Eleven

Five Magic Stones

If you're going to construct a building, you need a solid foundation. And if you're going to construct your life, you must have some strong pillars to weather the storms. You need a lot of pillars in life, but some are more vital to living a productive, healthy existence. Here are five that I feel will help you immensely:

Magic Stone #1: Enthusiasm

In 1997, I spoke to a group of eighth-graders in one of the best schools in America. There were 350 students in this grade, and nobody smiled when I greeted them and shook hands at the door as they came in. About a month later I had dinner with an eighth-grader from this school. Ironically, she had been absent that day, but I asked her why the students hadn't smiled. She said, "Because it isn't cool to smile." Of all the answers and comments I received from you over the last couple of years, this was the only one I was truly disturbed by. Here is the smile—the universal form of communication—and these students are saying it isn't cool to smile. People who have visited a foreign country where they couldn't speak the language found that they were totally dependent on their facial expressions, most significantly, the smile. And believe me, a smile can go a long way. Smiling and being enthusiastic sends out wonderful signals to people. You can do almost anything if you have enthusiasm. Enthusiasm is that sparkle in your eye or the grip in your hand. Simply put, enthusiasm is at the beginning of all progress. It is the ingredient so necessary to overcome disappointment. Tommy Lasorda, the manager of the Los Angeles Dodgers baseball team for so many years, said, "The best day of my life is when I manage a winning team. The second best day of my life is when I manage a losing team." Winston Churchill said, "Success is going from failure to failure without loss of enthusiasm."

Anybody can be enthusiastic when you're on top of the world and all is going well, but the key is to be enthusiastic even during times of struggle.

When you are with people who are enthusiastic, you are attracted to them like a magnet.

When you walk into a room for a job interview, most interviewers will look for your smile, particularly since most jobs today are in the service industry, where a smile is vital. Many interviewers say that they make the decision whether or not to hire you within the first two minutes, before you've even said much beyond "Hello."

If you are an enthusiastic person, it comes through immediately. When you meet someone with a smiling face, it says they have a grip on life. So if you are someone who does not smile naturally, practice in front of a mirror. Work with someone on videotape. We have a tennis professional in our company whom I met 20 years ago in an interview. I don't remember a single thing about that interview, but I do remember his smile, and so does everyone else. Our company has never had a complaint about him, in spite of the normal errors he makes in his job, like the rest of us. How can you get upset with someone with a warm, friendly, enthusiastic smile?

> "Of all the things you wear, your expression is the most important."

Magic Stone #2: Appreciation

I know we talked about this earlier, but appreciation is so much needed today that it can't be overemphasized. One of the quotes I heard when I was younger that really helped me is, "Always appreciate, never expect." Expectation sets you up for disappointment. As well, appreciation is one of the most needed human desires. Yet we don't do it enough. In fact, at funerals, most of the people who died unfortunately never heard the wonderful things that were said about them in the eulogies. For some strange reason, we have a lot easier time criticizing people than complimenting them.

I'm sure some of you reading this are saying, "That's my parents. They are always criticizing me." And you are probably right. A recent study of parent/teenager relationships found that there are 14 minutes of conversation between the average parent and teenager per day. Twelve minutes are negative, one minute neutral, and one minute positive. This is sad. You could take the initiative to change this. When I asked a number of you the question, "When was the last time you told your parents that they were doing a great job raising you?" many of you said you've never done that. Look at it from their perspective. If you spent 13 to 19 years doing something, seven days a week, 24 hours a day, and nobody patted you on the back, you wouldn't be in too positive a frame of mind either. This is what your parents go through. Even if you don't have the greatest of parents, you can always find some good things to tell them. Every parent has some good points. Compliment them on those points. Remember, some parents are insecure because they don't get any positive strokes from anywhere.

And what about your expectations versus appreciation? When you graduate from high school, you're probably expecting a graduation present from your parents, when in actuality it should be you giving the present to them. Think of all the sacrifices they have made to allow you to have this schooling. Both parents working—single parents working two jobs—saving money from the time you were born, etc.

And did you know that the custom used to be (and still is in some cultures) that on your birthday, you were the one who gave other people presents? You appreciated that you made it another year. Birthdays were a time of gratitude and generosity.

Perhaps the best thing you could do to show appreciation is to do something for your mom (if she is still with you) every time it is YOUR birthday. Think about the suffering, pain, sacrifice, and commitment that your mom made to give you this life. It could be a well-thought-out letter or a gift you made—just something that expresses your deep appreciation. Some of you may be wondering about your dad. He helped in the beginning, but it was your mom who carried you for the nine months prior to your birth. Doing something for your dad is important, but your mom really should be first on the appreciation list.

Or, let's say you've been working hard on taking responsibility and earning your parents' respect. If you get it, say thanks to them.

A number of you asked about the practice of killing turkeys on Thanksgiving and Christmas. In the U.S. alone, 67 million birds are slaughtered as we "give" thanks. You had trouble understanding the connection: a day of thanks and a day of joy being celebrated with the death of an innocent creature? To those of you who asked this question, I applaud your sensitivity. I don't understand it either.

In summation, learning to say thank you in a sincere, humble manner is one of your magic stones for having a happy, worthwhile life.

"Gratitude and inner peace go hand in hand."

Magic Stone #3: Respect

When people from a foreign country land in America, there are two things that are a culture shock. The first is the abundance of shopping malls, and the second is the children's lack of respect for their elders. In fact, there is a saying overseas that if kids in that country stop respecting their parents, they say they've become "Americanized." In almost all cultures and countries, since the beginning of time, the elders were the respected citizens. Today we ship off our sweet, kind-hearted grandmas and grandpas to old folks' homes while, on the other end of the spectrum, we cheer and adore 18 year olds who can put a ball through a hoop. The result of this loss of respect for elders in the family has increased to include the loss of respect for teachers, bosses, managers, coaches, and so on. And this leads to a loss of respect for ourselves.

In the final chapter I will address your health and the health of the planet. But here's a good time to point out that lack of respect for our land and all of life is part of our consciousness now. Showing respect is a sign of maturity and that you are secure with who you are. It is sad that when some of you genuinely want to thank your teachers and be respectful, your friends say you are "brownnosing."

When Hakeem Olajuwan came to the University of Houston from Africa, he bowed his head out of respect to those senior to him, and some of the American players laughed at him. When he left Africa his dad said, "Be careful, be respectful, be humble, and work hard." And very few can deny the great respect that Hakeem has garnered in return from his fans and his fellow NBA players.

Being respectful doesn't necessarily mean that you agree with what a person does. There was a very successful coach at UCLA named John Wooden in the 1960s and 70s. His star player was Bill Walton, who went on to star in the NBA for the Portland Trailblazers. Coach Wooden insisted on a player having short hair, and Bill Walton refused to cut his hair. Coach Wooden's response was very simple: "I have great respect for people who stand up for what they believe in, and I'm going to miss him."

I know that some of you have a hard time respecting your parents because of the way they act or the lifestyle they may lead. That's understandable. But your life will be a lot smoother if you respect the POSITION of a parent. You may not like your teachers, but respect that they are in charge. Someday you'll be in charge of people, and life is a series of circles. Whatever goes around, comes around.

"It always surprises me that otherwise intelligent people don't realize that if you treat people badly, it will eventually come back to you."

Charles Grodin - TV personality

"The new education must emphasize reverence for all life. All our ecological problems would be solved if only we grow in the spirit of reverence for all of life. All of life must be regarded as sacred."

Gandhi

Magic Stone #4: Being Positive

Since most of you reading this aren't married yet or having full-time jobs, this is a perfect time to share some advice on selecting people with whom you might spend a lot of time. Throughout this book I've been careful to avoid the word never, but I will now take liberty to use it, because I feel it is extremely important here. The advice is to do everything in your power to never marry or work with a negative or moody person. Ask anybody who has done this. You might even have a negative or moody parent. It's no fun, since you may find yourself gradually inching toward a negative spot on the mood barometer. Do your utmost to stop the slide. With everything in life, there is both a positive and a negative aspect. Successful people look at the positive side and focus on that. And if you sense yourself having mood swings toward a negative or unhappy thought process, develop a plan of action to counter this. For example, you may be feeling down, but when people ask you how you're doing, you respond, "Great, fantastic, thanks." Your brain is connected to every cell in your body, so your body becomes bathed in positiveness. The mind is so powerful that we can turn around how we feel very quickly. I am sure all of you have friends or family members who, when asked how they're doing, respond,

"Hanging in there," or "Not so good," or "Terrible" on a regular basis. Or there are those who say, "Not too bad," thereby implying that all days are bad, and this one just isn't "too" bad. After awhile, you don't want to ask them how they're doing, because they just bring you down.

Also, some people spend a good portion of their lives at the complaint counter. They're always finding something wrong. In fact, some teachers, coaches, and parents are like that. Instead of catching the kids doing something right, they spend a lot of time catching them doing things wrong. Parents play a major role in how their children view life. A very good friend of mine in Hawaii, Rob Thibaut, passed away from cancer in May 1998. At the funeral, his wife Patty spoke about two things that Rob focused on each night at dinner. Rob, Patty, and their three children talked about "the best thing that happened to them during the day." And secondly, Rob reinforced how much he loved each of them. My wife and I saw Rob's picture in a book before we met him many years ago, and we both said that he would be someone we would like to meet. His smile exuded such a positive outlook! He became one of my best friends. When we would be at a social function together, I would find myself trying to figure out how I could sit next to him.

Unfortunately, today we live in a predominantly negative society. For example, if you drive to work and there's a bad car wreck on one side and a magnificent sunrise on the other, guess which of the two events you will talk about when you get to work?

In today's world it's easy to be negative, where distressing information dominates the news. Couple this with the fact that we will be regularly wounded (physically, mentally, or emotionally), and being positive seems like a lot of work. Yet, you can turn your wounds into wisdom. As you gain knowledge in anything, you gain confidence.

Negative people have a couple of favorite phrases. "Yeah, but" and "That's impossible." You come up to a negative person and say, "Nice day today" and they say "Yeah, but it's going to rain." "Yeah but, yeah but, yeah but." Millions of dreams have been shot down because of these two words.

And how many parents have said to their children, "That's impossible, you could never accomplish that." Do yourself a favor. Throw the word 'impossible' into the verbal wastebasket. Getting on a positive channel will have a huge impact on both yourself and those around you. In every situation and in every person, look for the best part. You will see the difference it makes. Seek out your sources of positive energy.

"Things turn out best for those who make the best of the way things turn out."

"If you do not want to hit the bottom, stop digging the hole."

Magic Stone #5: Humility

Somewhere, sometime, somehow, part of the American psyche brought forth the concept of humility being equated with weakness. This is very unfortunate, as humility doesn't mean thinking less of yourself. It just means thinking of yourself less. In other words, you still have self-confidence, but you don't spend time telling everyone how great you are. This is where males have to work harder. Our humility doesn't usually come naturally. Growing up in America also doesn't help. You see high profile athletes pumping their chests and telling interviewers on TV how great they are. You hear politicians tell how much better your life will be if you vote for them. You see musicians soak up the adoration you give them and then shun you when you want their autographs.

The end result is that you think you have to be forward, arrogant, and self-serving in order to do well. You get a false sense of how good you really are.

I always enjoy seeing the global exam contest given to students in different countries around the world.

This is where teenagers represent their countries and compete scholastically against their peers from other parts of the world. The Americans, when asked where they will finish, proudly proclaim, "First." And each year they usually finish last—an experience that should be a humbling one.

We need failures to keep us humble. If you are already successful as a teenager in some field, you need someone to keep it in perspective for you. Yannick Noah was a top ten professional tennis player in the 1970s and 1980s. He came from Cameroon in Africa and played for France. I ran into him on an island in St. Bart's after he had retired, and he told me, "With all the money and admiration, you begin to think you are special instead of someone who is just lucky."

A person who is successful in any endeavor, yet who doesn't brag about it, is greatly admired and respected. Be as good as you are, but avoid feeling that you are superior to others.

I often get asked what is the most important quality a person should have. Without hesitation I answer, "Humility." Because if you are humble, you will always be willing to learn. And if you are willing to learn, you will have more knowledge. And with knowledge will come understanding. And with understanding will come the confidence to make a difference.

Dear Teenager

In life there are obviously more than just five magic stones, but these are the 'biggies.' Work on these, and the world around you will change overnight. I promise.

> "The value of a life is not measured by the number of your possessions, but by the time spent giving of yourself."

Chapter Twelve

Your Health

Without good health, you may find most of this book is pretty irrelevant. In *USA Weekend*'s survey on teenagers, 89 percent of you considered yourself physically healthy. Yet in reality, this is not true. We have seen some of your peers die of heart attacks before they were 20. A large majority of you is overweight. An even higher percentage of you don't have a lot of energy and would rather channel surf the TV then do a physical activity.

Adults are saying, "Kids are so lazy today." They talk about how they walked to school, while you are driven or drive yourself to school. Yet they hardly ever look at their generation as the cause of this. How many parents buy you a car and then say how lazy you are? How many have sold or bought products that have made the world a lot more dangerous, necessitating that you being driven to school? And look at the food many of you have been brought up on. Your parents feed you junk food when you are toddlers and wonder why healthy food isn't appealing to you later on. They distort your tastebuds with fats and sugars when you are young and then think you can switch gears on your food choices overnight.

In today's overprocessed, stressed out, polluted world, a good diet is essential. Yet, less than one percent of teenagers has a healthy diet (*Pediatric Magazine*).

Your food is your fuel. Pure honey is a tasty substance, but if you put it in the gas tank of your car, your car won't work. Our bodies require the right fuels, and we aren't supplying them.

In order to supply foods that hurt us, we in turn rape our land and pollute our air and water. It's fascinating that on one hand scientists are trying to make us healthy with drugs and, on the other hand, killing us with pollution. Today's environment places a tremendous strain on our bodies. We are constantly battling against invading chemicals that weaken our body's defenses. And you wonder why you feel so tired in school. When your defense system is weakened, you get tired and lethargic. How many of you feel like concentrating in school right after you've had lunch? How inspired are you to do your homework after dinner when your body is tired? Most of what you eat today places such a strain on your body that you just aren't motivated. And it's the adults who then say, "Our kids just aren't motivated these days."

And what about the mental anxiety created by being surrounded with violence? We don't respect the life of all creatures. Every year over eight billion animals are slaughtered so we can satisfy our learned craving for a substance that physiologically doesn't belong in our bodies.

Are you aware of the millions of creatures that are imprisoned in tiny cages, deprived of fresh air, of movement, of light, forced to stand in their own filth all their lives? Are you aware that animals are being stunned as they enter the slaughterhouse and hung upside down, waiting for their throats to be cut? And this nightmare goes on, day after day, for millions of creatures, who would prefer to die than live in conditions of which the Nazi concentration camps would be ashamed.

I advise all of you to visit a slaughterhouse. When I first went, I was extremely upset with myself for being so ignorant of what goes on behind those four windowless walls. Ask if you can take pictures. Most slaughterhouses won't allow you to, because they don't want the masses of people to know where those cellophane-packaged containers of red meat actually come from or the horrific process of getting them there.

Most females are inherently more sensitive and will be stunned when they see how the animals' lives are taken away. Some males will be salivating at the thought of their next hamburger or breast of chicken. But it takes a very insensitive person to not be affected by this experience. Our bodies are physiologically not designed to handle meat, fish, chicken, and eggs. By consuming them, we extract an enormous toll on our energy level while trying to get these substances through our bodies. The subject is far too complex to do justice to, so I suggest you read my book called *Total Health* (Torchlight Publishing).

However, here are just a few thoughts to consider. All societies were vegetarian in the beginning. As the societies become more affluent, they added the meats. And as they added the meats, they got the affluent lifestyle diseases (heart attack, high blood pressure, cancer, osteoporosis, and obesity). The latter lifestyle disease, obesity, concerns many teenagers. And justifiably so.

When I grew up, there was one fat boy in our class. He had a terrible time because he was teased so much. Today I haven't seen classrooms with just one fat person. In fact, a person who is actually fit and in good shape is the rarity and is perceived as skinny. Our society is fat—way too fat. And as a teenager, this isn't fun. We talked about insecurity. You can be the nicest person in the class, be intelligent and hardworking, but if you are overweight, your self-esteem takes a huge nose-dive.

In talking to students at their schools for a number of years now, I do not have a word that describes my shock and disappointment at the food options in your cafeterias at school. And what you were taught (or not taught) about nutrition? The board of health has been duped by the corporate world. And who are the losers? YOU.

Most people who have studied obesity accept that in only occasional circumstances is obesity genetic. You look at your mom and dad who are overweight and think you've got it from them. The problem, in fact, is that you have been eating at the same dinner table for many years now. You have expanded together. They are just bigger because they have been eating the wrong foods longer than you have.

Anorexia and bulimia are hot topics. They happen because of a lack of understanding of WHAT to eat. They don't exist in societies and cultures where food choices are appropriate for the body. Such drastic measures are totally unnecessary. If you come to understand and make proper food choices, anorexia and bulimia will pretty much disappear from the scene.

A major challenge for teenagers is educating your parents. I've witnessed a great many of you teenagers make a concerted effort to eat better. You have made the choice because you want to be healthier, or because, morally, you respect the animals' lives, or ecologically speaking, you want to help heal the planet. You are full of enthusiasm and committed to the change, and what happens? Your parents sabotage your sincere efforts. They say, "It's just a fad." "You'll grow out of it." "You'll get sick." "Where are you going to get your protein?" "You've flipped out." "As long as you live under my roof, you'll eat whatever I serve you."

Instead of trying to learn from you, understand you, and respect your decision, they go on the attack. And you dig in your heels, because you've learned something and want to change. You know better. Unfortunately, another family argument arises.

Adults generally make lifestyle changes because of health reasons first and moral reasons second, ecological reasons third. With teenagers it's a toss up between ecological and moral reasoning being their first choice, with health in third place. This is very commendable, particularly regarding the moral reasoning. If you change because of the moral reasons, you will most likely remain committed. Those doing it just for health reasons tend to cheat and fall back.

Since you teenagers have been handed the fractured, unhealthy planet Earth, many of you are deeply concerned. Your concern is commendable for two reasons. It helps you focus on something more important and bigger than you and, secondly, we need your direction and leadership.

The two generations before you have messed it up big time. So many of them are making money at the expense of (y)our planet. The motivation to heal it just isn't there. So it's up to you. It's been extremely gratifying to see how seriously you have taken up the banner to repair the planet and to look beyond your own limited world. A great example of this is World Vision's 30-hour famine program, where 600,000 teenagers fast for 30 hours to raise money to combat global hunger. In addition, they are conducting two million hours of community service in an effort to show adults that they really do care and sincerely want to be part of solving the world's challenges and problems.

Perhaps the biggest contribution you can make now is to understand how making good food choices will be the most powerful step you can take ecologically. It's not easy, because there's an enormous dependency of the American economy on the exploitation of animals. In addition, even though the U.S. has less than five percent of the world's population, the country uses 33 percent of the world's reserves and causes 50 percent of the industrial pollution.

In many ways, because of the effect America has on the rest of the world (both good and bad), American teenagers can and probably will be the leaders in the turnaround.

All the 8,400,000 species of life are intertwined. By respecting all of life (not just humans), by respecting your home, the planet, and by respecting your own health, you will see magical things happen. For generations it's been said that teenagers are our future. Never before has this been more true. Not only are you our future, but you will be the ones altering the way we live. You are our captains and pilots.

> "To my mind, the life of a lamb is no less precious than the life of a human being. I should be unwilling to take the life of a lamb for the sake of the human body. I hold that the more helpless a creature, the more entitled it is to protection by man from cruelty."
>
> Mahatma Gandhi

> "Our civilization lacks humane feeling. We are humans who are insufficiently humane. We have lost sight of this ideal because we are solely occupied with thoughts of men, instead of remembering that our goodness and compassion should extend to all creatures, for their health, not just ours."
>
> Dr. Albert Schweitzer

Closing

When I was in Shanghai, China a few years ago, I was asked by a gentleman to autograph the first book I wrote, called *Tennis for Life*. It was the original version, which had been banned in China because there were pictures of one of our female tennis professionals in a regular tennis dress. However, in China, books were not allowed where there were photos of females with the hemline of the skirt above the knee. This book had been smuggled all the way up from Hong Kong, and this individual was thrilled to meet the author.

Around this time, I was wondering whether I should write more books. This experience convinced me to keep writing. Even though I thoroughly disliked reading and writing when I was in school, I now love the experience. Part of the joy of writing a book is to share knowledge. But the best part is hearing how the books have helped or changed people's lives. Therefore, I would greatly appreciate it if you could take the time to write me and share how your life was altered because of something you read in this book.

Closing

The goal is then to do a follow-up of this book with a series of success stories. The purpose is to have you, as the future leaders, share your stories so that others can be motivated by what happened to you. We will select the best stories for the next book and may contact you for some additional details.

A candle loses nothing by passing on light to another candle, so I look forward to reading your story.

May I officially close by expressing to you my sincere thanks for coming on this journey. I have learned a lot from you.

Exploding the myths of America's diet and exercise programs!

"Read *Total Health* and heed its wise and compassionate counsel, and you will be well on the way to a new level of aliveness, healing, and joy."

—from the Foreword by John Robbins, author of *Diet for a New America* and Founder of EarthSave International

"Peter Burwash really hits the nail on the head. This book is terrific and long overdue."

—Ingrid E. Newkirk, President of PETA

"If anyone is qualified to write a book on health, it is Peter Burwash — athlete, philosopher, lover of life, and one of the healthiest people I've ever met. This sage guidance on achieving total health is a gift — for your body, for your spirit, and for the health of the entire planet."

—Michael A. Klaper, M.D., author of *Vegan Nutrition, Pure and Simple*

Take charge of your life!

$12.95
ISBN #1-887089-15-2
5"x 7", cloth
128 pages

"A blend of practical wisdom and a depth of experience to teach us how to take charge of every aspect of our lives."
—from the Foreword by Lee Iacocca

Improving the Landscape of Your Life offers a fresh and practical approach to achieving new levels of personal effectiveness.

Peter Burwash reveals twelve essential habits for succeeding and understanding true happiness.

The happiest people are those who try to help others and who don't necessarily have the best of everything, but they make the best of everything they have.

Although Peter's book is presented in bite-sized chapters, don't let its size fool you. Inside you'll find twelve very powerful and practical lessons on how to take charge of every aspect of your life.

Book Order Form ─────────

☎ Telephone orders: Call 1-888-TORCHLT (1-888-867-2458)
    Please have your credit card ready.
✳ Fax orders: 559-337-2354
✉ Postal orders: Torchlight Publishing, P. O. Box 52, Badger, CA 93603-0052, USA

▲ World Wide Web: www.torchlight.com

Please send the following:

The Key to Great Leadership	$11.95 X_____	= $_____
Total Health: The Next Level	$11.95 X_____	= $_____
Improving the Landscape of Your Life	$12.95 X_____	= $_____
Dear Teenager, If You Only Knew . . .	$12.95 X_____	= $_____

Sales tax (CA residents add 7.25%) $_____
Shipping and handling (see below) $_____
TOTAL $_____

○ **Please send me your catalog and info on other books by Torchlight Publishing**

Company_____
Name_____
Address_____
City _____ State_____ Zip_____

(I understand that I may return any books for a full refund—no questions asked.)

Payment:

○ Check / money order enclosed   ○ VISA   ○ MasterCard   ○ American Express
    Card number_____
    Name on card_____ Exp. date_____
    Signature_____

Shipping and handling: Book rate: USA $2.00 for first book, $1.00 for each additional book.
Canada: $3.00 for first book, $2.00 for each additional book. Foreign countries: $4.00 for first book,
$3.00 for each additional book. (Surface shipping may take 3–4 weeks. Foreign orders please allow
6–8 weeks for delivery.)